T0004875

Sometimes We Feel
Angry

By Emiliya King

Cavendish Square

New York

Published in 2022 by Cavendish Square Publishing, LLC
243 5th Avenue, Suite 136, New York, NY 10016

Copyright © 2022 by Cavendish Square Publishing, LLC

First Edition

Library of Congress Cataloging-in-Publication Data

Names: King, Emiliya, author.
Title: Sometimes we feel angry / Emiliya King.
Description: New York : Cavendish Square Publishing, [2022] | Series: Dealing with your feelings | Includes index.
Identifiers: LCCN 2020030631 | ISBN 9781502659880 (library binding) | ISBN 9781502659866 (paperback) | ISBN 9781502659873 (set) | ISBN 9781502659897 (ebook)
Subjects: LCSH: Anger in children–Juvenile literature. | Anger–Juvenile literature.
Classification: LCC BF723.A4 P494 2022 | DDC 155.4/1247–dc23
LC record available at https://lccn.loc.gov/2020030631

Editor: Caitie McAneney
Designer: Deanna Paternostro

The photographs in this book are used by permission and through the courtesy of: Cover Casezy idea/Shutterstock.com; p. 5 Johner Images/Getty Images; p. 7 skynesher/E+/Getty Images; p. 9 fizkes/iStock/Getty Images Plus/Getty Images; pp. 11, 17 JGI/Jamie Grill/Getty Images; p. 13 kkay/E+/Getty Images; p. 15 Wavebreakmedia/iStock/Getty Images Plus/Getty Images; p. 19 Nick David/Stone/Getty Images; p. 21 MoMo Productions/DigitalVision/Getty Images; p. 23 Tom Werner/DigitalVision/Getty Images.

Some of the images in this book illustrate individuals who are models. The depictions do not imply actual situations or events.

CPSIA compliance information: Batch #CS22CSQ: For further information contact Cavendish Square Publishing LLC, New York, New York, at 1-877-980-4450.

Printed in the United States of America

Find us on

CONTENTS

What Is Anger?

Have you ever felt angry?
Sometimes we feel mad.
We feel things are not fair.
We feel someone has hurt us.
We feel **upset**. This big, bad
feeling is anger.

You might feel angry if you don't get what you want. You might want ice cream. However, your mom makes you a salad instead. You might want to play, but your dad says it's time for bed.

7

You might feel angry if
someone hurts you. You might
be hurt if you're picked last
for a team. You might be hurt
if you're left out. You might
be hurt if someone says
something mean to you.

9

How It Feels

What does anger feel like in your body? Your face might get hot. You might start to shake. Your heart might start to race. You might frown and cross your arms. You might even cry.

Anger tells your body it's time to fight. Anger can make you feel like yelling or saying something mean. It can make you feel like pushing or hitting. Sometimes acting out makes your anger feel even stronger.

Dealing with Anger

Everyone feels angry sometimes. However, acting on anger is hurtful. It can make you hurt yourself and others. It can even get you in big trouble! It's important to learn how to deal with hard feelings.

14

15

What should you do when you feel angry? First, take a deep breath. Breathe in and out slowly. You can close your eyes or sit down. It's important to **calm** down before you act.

Anger often gives you a lot of **energy**. You might think hitting something is the only way to use this energy. However, you can run or walk. You can draw, write, or sing. Use your energy for good!

19

Are you calm? Now you can think clearly. Ask yourself why you were angry. Was something unfair? Were you hurt? Think about how you can fix the problem. Ask an adult for help if you don't know what to do.

You don't have to lose your **temper**. Use your words instead of yelling or hitting. You might say, "I was angry because I wasn't given a turn. It hurt my feelings." You are more than your anger!

23

WORDS TO KNOW

calm: A feeling of peace.

energy: The power to work or to act.

temper: A strong feeling, usually having to do with anger.

upset: Troubled.

INDEX